# Moth Moon

## Matt Jasper

**BlazeVOX** [books]

Buffalo, New York

BlazeVOX [books]
303 Bedford Ave
Buffalo, NY 14216


Editor@blazevox.org

*publisher of weird little books*

# BlazeVOX [ books ]

blazevox.org

2    4    6    8    0    9    7    5    3    1

# Table of Contents

# Moth Moon

## FLIGHT

In the field, birds rising black against the sun.
You say they are ravens. They should be careful.
If one of them opens its wings too wide
all of the light in the world will be blotted out forever.

## ANASTASIA, PURDY GROUP HOME

A man has entered the room.
He is a ladykiller. A real one:
growing smaller and larger and more wonderful and terrible.
His stomach opens, the room fills
with ladykillers.
They are eating you up with their eyes.

The nurse gives you twenty milligrams of Haldol.
Most of the ladykillers leave but there is one left.
You point to him and say, "I get carried away,"
meaning that he has come to steal you.

Anastasia, on this night
you pass out half a carton of cigarettes
and tell me that you will not live
to see another day.

At nine in the morning I try to wake you.
I say your name, I rock you back and forth.
You open one eye
and say, "what you touching my hip bone for,
you going to make soup?"

You are pleased to meet me.
May you ask who I am?
Am I your parent or savior?
a husband? Do I think
you will be a melt-as-you-go-wife?

Anastasia, you are beautiful:
rotten teeth, rosary beads, the dresses you wear when you sleep.
I will give you your Haldol, your Xanax
an hour late.
We will walk to the store for more cigarettes.

## MOTH MOON

A man who has worn away his hair
against the pillow by shaking
his head
No.

The man who stands over him
whispering secrets of poisonous snow.

A woman who suffers from Dutch elm disease,
who speaks to her hands as they turn to dried leaves
falling
outside the window—
her hands covering the ground.

The porch light snaps on.
The man
who had wandered away now appears:
smoking his cigarette,
watching.

The insects gather. The moths
have finally found their moon.
Here on earth, wings burning.
Bodies falling slowly, like ashes
they had hoped they would rise from.

# A TRANSLATION, PURDY GROUP HOME

Know that girl in the green sweater?
He ate her.
Had chicken in his mouth
then only a bone.
They say it's lions' heads he keeps in his refrigerator—
It's people.

I die easily in here.
I need help for my hands.
Showers kill easily.
My head spins around at times.
I notice that I am about to stand
and through God (with hatred enough at times)
I am killed over and over again.
I am standing in the place and the place changes.
I am the changing of the place.

# RORSCHACH TEST

I call this green ink blot
in the shape of a bear
"grass bear."
*

This is an eagle
being blown apart by a bullet
or by the wind.
*

The antlers of a doe flying on a red sunset.
Her secret, right
here. It's how she makes the babies.
*

Mice playing.
It means the cat is away.
Means tiny footprints:
feet of adultery upon the clean floor.
*

A dog rearing on its haunches.
He has eaten a gravy-soaked sponge.
He leaves no footprints and soon the other animals
can see only his black teeth.
*

The man on the window ledge.
*

The air is still here—
the air between the things in the room.
But the things themselves
have disappeared.
*

Like the river.
The water and a snake going up to the sky.
That's bad luck—
a snake going up to the sky for a river.

# TEACHING COOKING SKILLS, PURDY GROUP HOME

These are the ovens of the dead
who fall from each cabinet we open.
See them rising
as bread rises,
see them empty themselves
as an ingredient
or lie before us peacefully saying
*This is my body which is broken for you,*
*this is my blood which you stir.*

The food in our mouths was their food long ago.
They are filling us with deadness
so we can follow them to where they show us
their perfect kitchens that gleam without
the sorrow of these wings cut off and packaged
so we can roll them in the flour.

## MATHEMATICIAN

Dismembered figures taking form from the page they were calculated on. The unending geometry of his salvation. Body counts that rise as he holds the wrong belief. Or uses the product of a manufacturer who does not obey the Ten Commandments. Small open graves reflected in his spoon. Causing him to rise from his seat. Causing him to say, 'May the slaughtered sheep of my kingdom come forth and be redeemed. May their redemption be measured in complimentary sets of silverware.' For he wanders through the streets calling out his own name. For someone has subtracted him from a calculation he will never see. For he approaches a woman who viciously denies that her breasts are billowing zeppelins, that her eyes. They are so blue.

## YELLOW LINE

David D. 33 of Manchester eats with his face in his plate and screams Manchester eats with his face in his plate and screams for his face in his plate for no apparent reason. Police charged him with disorderly conduct for pounding nails into the yellow line on a busy city street. He is often arrested for misdemeanor crimes associated with his mental illness and problems with his face in his plate. At least two psychiatrists and a psychologist have examined David for no apparent reason often screams for his face in his plate pounds nails into himself and others is dangerous to the yellow line.

## DIVINING

God finally destroys the devil and accidentally disappears. I steal the bread of understanding and cast it to the duck pond. I have done what is good until an old and wise mallard looks me coldly in the eye, whispers that I have caused overpopulation, eventual starvation. It occurs to me that I give to charity only so calf-eyed children can continue to lead quiet lives.

The urge to go on a three state killing spree. Or help an old lady to cross the street. The realization that any action has an equal and opposite reaction, that to do any one thing is to kill the other. Parts of my body crawl away and are never seen again. I win friends. Their limbs fold back into a tree that leaves no seed. A tree that begs me to eat its red fruit. A tree that tells me the road to hell is paved with ordinary asphalt.

## RELATIONSHIP

I am to the window as the window is to the man
who has turned to face it.

It follows that I will not jump from the window
and that the window will not jump from me.

This is our agreement.

## SEED

*I was whispering to my mother*
*only I was my father*
*only inside him*
*before he was born.*

A pair of legs wrapped in a towel
in the home for the unwhole, the way a dying tree
can sometimes escape through the seed that falls.
My name is called but already what must be believed
to be seen, is believed, is seen: a moon
wandering over the landscapes of all that it cannot love.

# FUSILLADE

Shells are eating away at the last angels perched
in the masonry of their building's façade.
However much they want to fly,
they stand there denying their insides
lie strewn across the downtown battlefield park
where embarrassed soldiers spend their time holding still
in sniper fire or posing for the monuments already being erected
to those stalwart heroes dragging their intestines
behind them like fishing nets trawling for new boots,
cigarettes, a little diary with burning pages
of love for the pregnant girl back home
who says she'll stagger in to this sad scene even
if it means stepping on mines that loft her
into the sky rolling past on a painted canvas scroll
cranked by horse-drawn turnstile or
a stationery bicyclist lying flat on his scented page
hoping the erasure of one spoke will be followed
by the sketching in of another.
This is how movement is created,
he will tell himself—
how celluloid cells advance through sprockets
toward the image they project, how we shudder
toward the ideas we have of ourselves until they light then leave us
bereft, yet not quite so lost as the pregnant girl
now returning to earth through the smoke
of the diary that burns for her
until enough of her spatters down to put it out.

# VENUS AT THE SHELL STATION

She passes from car to lot seamlessly—
The dream of a woman met and bedded down—
Her gown of a long T-shirt bulging
With my seed turned to melon.

She grows smaller as she walks away
To pay for gas and pretzels, to get the key
She needs to complete her disappearance.

One wave and she's gone, a closed door
Labeled "adies"
To project my visions of her upon.
How appropriate that it's dented
Yet otherwise working fine—
Her broad smile beaming
Amidst wreckage of moments that might
Flit about her like invisible flies
Swatted at by the mad.

She was hit, yes—
And addressed unkindly.
Sometimes she wished the gun her father held
Against his or perhaps her mother's head
Might go off.  In magnificent sunlight,
The finest scene must have been
That time her tiny family huddled inside
The sparkling shower of every window smashed
From station wagon by hammer—his raised hand
An exponent to her age.

When the glass was gone, he simply walked away—
Bearer of a torch of rage passed through generations
Right up to this moment at this station
Of whatever cross she carries.
I am wondering if she'll beat our child
When I notice how she walks with ease—
Her calloused feet hovering over pebbles,
Wrappers, and broken glass.
With each step they form an uncursed path.
I tell her she should have worn shoes.
She laughs.

## LULL

A son unwinds furnace-cheeked—
fists rubbing sleep into eyes amidst
wailing against the wailing
against the wailing wells that fill
like an upturned umbrella, a throat
opened wider than its voice can spill.

Little mirror we pour ourselves into—
emptied shoe fast asleep crying laces.
Your clothes are strewn where you
tumbled out of them to nest insistent
that the floor by the radiator
was the only place you could be.

I must lift you to the darker room—
set you down as gently as I used to set
half-walnut shells into a slow stream.
They would become boats if I was as careful
as I am now to let you sleep—
your voyage as winding and uncertain
as any shell that could bob along
or run aground on a bed.

Almost capsized by fever's twitch
or the wakening of puckered lips nursing
on some huge invisible breast—
I bequeath you my awe for potential power
lying dormant.
Whether landslide, eye of storm,
tiny volcano or tectonic plate—
from the tea of recovery
I raise my cup to you quite shaken.

# EUDORA

She sets a tea for seen and unseen guests—
Empty chairs and stuffed pets.
She pours and talks from place to place.

By way of apology to the Easter Bunny
She says, "And Grampa Widdy will be here too
When he stops being DEAD."

She sort of sneers that last line—
Rolls her eyes and shifts her hips
As if she's bored and seventeen.

Yes, death is a minor inconvenience
That keeps one from attending tea parties
Until by special excavation they are cordially invited.

Those who in their poor taste died before Eudora could turn three
Must attend unendingly.
Must bend, must bow, must drink their tea.

# TRIBUTARY

Aged two and three—
they seal-slide toward the sunlit top
of a stream that froze then lowered
a foot to freeze again beneath
its higher ceiling.

Their father startles then recalls
it's been cold too long for them to be taken
by the water beneath. Cautious
of caution, he sends
no warning to the delighted pair
as they smash through sparkling almost-glass
and discover these things:

They are still alive; they never knew
there could be ice beneath ice, that something thin
could smash them down to something holding firm
the memory that it once babbled and soaked.

By lying on their backs and pushing with their heels,
they can just fit under the sheet—
looking up through a craggy lens into a smeared sky
of lit branches iced also into conspiracy
smashed by laughter as sons destroy
the glory of a quarter mile—sliding under like torpedoes
slowed by the lifting shark fin of a knee.

When they see that propelling themselves cracks the sky,
they flatten and lie there chewing watery shards,
spitting out wool mitten fibers, demanding
that he push them farther than he dares—
each time closer and closer to beyond
where he hopes they will rise up
and return to him only
to be launched farther away.

When at last they slide
then creep around a bend
and don't come back to him,
he learns to trust that their screams
are joyous though reminiscent
in pitch to those of eviscerated swine.
The stream is frozen, he reminds himself.
There's no need to tell them not to get carried away.

## ANNIVERSARY

If a harbor then a shore,
if implored
then given freely—
by feel as along a banister
swaying beneath the weight of hands that slide along.

If returned to, then once abandoned
by those whose clothes were worn and wore out
until implied meant afraid to say
like charges repel, electrostatic repugnance,
fleas jumping from the executed man....

One flea is always on the way back
to the betrothed betrayed.

If love, then a shiver of recognition
air-conditioned through ductwork of dull days
and petty bickering—
a slammed door
left standing as the house around it falls.

My love of many days forgotten—
We slip away unaware—too familiar to be seen
until our noticing shows us (hair flowing without faucet
down curves that welcome, skin worn
into a map of the years)

we must have been away.

## FALL

Owl left branch to warn you—
this is the misery of hands
thrown up in despair.

At first only a pair yet one feels
what they clutched at,
caressed.

The warmth remaining
is best remembered
as leaves fall, we gather them—

A harvest which lies unused as
hands contract the disease of falling
with the weight of all they've touched.

The leaves are hands falling past brooms
and rakes now falling too
and we, upon them

completed
not by falling but
by what all falling is toward.

## ECLIPSE

The children gnaw, they love her,
they're good. They gnaw and I gnaw too.
She loves us—the gnawing
can't be helped. It's as if
it's a form of love. The baby wakes up
saying *Hey Mom, I want candy!*
His mother half-laughs but it's 5 a.m.
and the unfolded laundry reminds her
of the months she's gone without seeing
her washing machine. She yells
to one child who tells the others—
*Mom said to get dressed with the tides
and wash your hair with a golden cloth.*

How far this is
from what she said—
how they turn her words
into something better—the way they smile at first
not believing they could ever be screamed at.
She would take her words back, blame herself
more than she should. She's good to them
when she's there to embrace, turn
pages, or gather sweaters and braid hair
for a trip to the ocean.

Yet she's been lying here nailed in place.
While the youngest shakes her
everyone else is in the kitchen.
In a way, the distance
is good for them (she thinks—
in case she has to leave).

They open cupboards in search of jam
and chocolate chips, or assemble
an almond omelette breakfast easily eclipsing
anything I, their father, could create unaided.
While they work, I gather medicine from
the highest cupboards they can't reach—
in order to hide it from the one who can.
No car keys or rope either, someone to watch her, *hell—
it's not so hard.*
Even the hungry baby has her pinned down again—
patting her awake with his chubby hands.

# TONIGHT THEY MEET HER IN THE PARK

Fog erases the outlines of every streetlamp—
leaving lights suspended to glow not knowing
what holds them up is gone.

The man sits because his
legs have fallen away.

His children scatter bread
that is carried into the sky.
They lie on their backs and look
for clouds shaped like their mother.
This disease is harder on her,
he's sure.

The dog tells her what to do
when she bursts  into bits of light.
She might look back with eyes that aren't her own
or sob at the gowns of herself
she hangs upon the line.

*To dry after dying all day*
*is hard work,* she says.

She's seeing other people now
and can't do laundry and can't stay in
or a humming that's not just in her head
might begin to compose them all into its song—

*The weak are wrong*
*to be so weak. You see,*
*they ask for it on bended knee.*
*They fall prey*
*to the little things of the day.*

Maybe it's the dancing of those little things
on the tightening drum of her skin that makes
the humming begin.

It's bad for the children
to know their singing and shrieks
make their mother go.

Did they notice
she was gone, then returning
to the size of an ant, a worry doll, a cat,
a woman walking back for one evening hour
into who she used to be?

They are careful to search her eyes—
looking for clouds, candy,
collapsed cities, the thing inside
that makes her disappear.
Or worse, vanish
while still here.

## ESTRANGE

A final embrace tries to contain the years we spent together.
I walk you out. You turn to me
and say, "It seems like we could get into the car
and drive back into our old lives.
Our apartment would be just the way it was.
We would be waiting for ourselves there."

I didn't care when you left.
I laughed at everything and remembered you
only in dreams of sad trees.
They could not go on.
Their leaves had fallen.

They are coming back to me now—
the leaves of all of the leaves in the world.
Though they return, they return without you—
as I returned accidentally today
to our old driveway not remembering
until I looked up into the empty windows
that we were no longer there.

## BURIAL

She whispers—The ocean
is a stone's throw deep.
Her floating hands are the skeleton of a leaf.
We look into her eyes.
We find there are clouds.
They have risen from where the sun dies
into water at night.
The rain
falls faster and faster.
We feel it less and less.

# THE TIP OF THE ICEBERG

She calls every year before Christmas to say
She will never call again.  She's going away
To visit friends—all doctors and nurses
Who are secretly in love with her—
Who would like to line their gloves with her skin
Or pull out her eyes to see where she has been walking at night
Beneath the root of all trees, in the fields
Of the fatherless where everyone is practicing to die.
They jump into the air.  They fall
And jump again.

The one who never returns is the one who wins
Every prize there has ever been
For not returning—

To a Sicilian mother and a one-eyed cat,
To an attic apartment where every day her lifeless
Body was found in a different position—
Drinking a cup of coffee,
Cooking a meal for one.

Her new Camaro could be mine if I would marry her.
I hated Camaros and politely declined.

That Summer I was flattered to hear
She was committed for wanting to kill me.
I thought of her as I walked beneath the flowering trees
Thinking an assassin would be lovely on a night like this—
Someone to crouch beneath the porch with a rifle
Or wait in the tall grass for me to walk by.

Though I am not the archangel who breaks into her
House and spits on her bed, this is what
I remember of what she said—

*I was over her house that night.*
*This is how it began:*
*I was over her house because there were people in my room.*
*There were all of these people in my bedroom,*
*okay?*

*Not real people,*
*imaginary people.*
*There were people in my bedroom*
*so I made the mistake of sharing this fact with Cheryl,*
*who is a travel agent—*
*Cheryl Meyersen,*
*my best friend of eight years who lives at fifteen Temple Street*
*where it all began.*

*Then I was crying*
*and in tears*
*and she said (I can't remember telling her)*
*that I told her I wanted to kill you.*
*And I said I'm going to kill him,*
*I want to kill him.*
*And she and her mother took me to Saint Elizabeth's in Brighton*
*and I was really annoyed because they couldn't understand a thing*
*I was saying.*
*I couldn't even sit*
*in a little room because their presence annoyed me.*

*Cheryl Meyersen.*
*After I left the room Cheryl Meyersen and her mother had an*
*interview with the psychiatrist and he asked, well,*
*do you think she could hurt herself or someone else?*
*And Cheryl said that I wanted to kill you*
* so they had to commit me*
*because I'm a killer.*
*I'm a killer!*

*So, basically, Cheryl Meyersen—*
*she's known me for eight years and she thinks*
* I'm going to kill someone.*
*That's how well she knows me and that's why*
*she doesn't believe in ghosts*
*and she doesn't believe in anything*
*but she won't go down cellar by herself.*

*She says she is afraid of ghosts.*

*I said Cheryl, I thought you said you don't believe in them*
*and she said Daniel has to come downstairs with her.*

*So she has all this in her and she has to put ME away.*
*And her husband is an alcoholic!*
*And all his problems he was bringing into her*
*life for eight years. Anyway,*
*they are supposed to get married on November eleventh.*
*Two people I know already did get married on November*
*eleventh*
*and Jim's birthday is on November eleventh.*
*It's just basically a lot of coincidences and unfortunately*
*I'm Sicilian*
*and I have superstitions I carry around with me and you know*
*they make me a little crazy.*

*People realize this and they want to lock me up.*
*What I should probably do is quit my job and become an actress.*
*Oh, I did acting for a number of years, you know.*
*I was appealing to the masses then.*
*I played Amelia Earhart,*
*Dorothy in Oz.*

*Today I go to the Emerald Square Mall and buy ruby red slippers.*
*Well,*
        *I'm getting ready to sing in subways.*

*I was putting all these songs in manila folders*
*because I need to read the notes*
*because I can't memorize songs*
*and I only did Christmas stuff.*
*I only want to do Christmas stuff.*
*This will be after I move,*
*after Thanksgiving. So anyway,*
*I got a new guitar case.*
*Let me tell you about this place I went into.*
*I am an actress.*
*You will know this*
*when I tell you this story:*

*So,*
*on one side*
*here's this huge black aisle*
*like this.*
*On this side there are guns—*

all guns, ammunition, AK 47s,
whatever the heck,
everything.

On this side are guitars—
all guitar stuff.

So me and this guy I had this date with—
the total monk. After we had cappuccino at, um,
Cafe Pompeii—
which is the total mob hangout in the North End, I know
because I know the big mobsters in the North End personally
and they tell me all of their stories.
I've had mobsters tell me everything.
I mean everything. Well,
everything they had a need to confess—
like after freebasing cocaine and like, drinking.
Mobsters have a lot they want to get off their chest,
you know.
So anyway,
this man was behind a counter.
First he was selling someone a gun
then that same guy came from behind that counter.
This was in the heart of the North End!
—And walked around to this counter and helped me
and I was like, I want to buy a guitar case
and all this stuff innocently enough
and then I loved his voice!
I was telling him about what's wrong
with my guitar case and he said
Oh, really?
Just like that.
Can you imagine?
He was just like Oh,
really, is that so?
And I was like,
Yeah.

Can you imagine?

And after that all of the people from the North End—
like the low, little people who are trying to enter....
They have been coming to me for two days.
I've been bombarded by young men lookin for all sorts
of things.
I'm very much invaded.
People in the North End love me
and they come to visit me.
All of these people are coming to me for jobs
and they are coming from the North End.
I'm helping the people from the North End.
They have taken a very big liking to me.

They know me because they know my father.
All of the big mobsters in the North End know my father.
You know how I know?
—They offer me their hand.
In the North End I lose my wallet
and they return it to me with all the money still in it.
It's because of my father.
He was the only one who would let me sing whenever I wanted.
He was a mass murderer.

I think he was the Boston strangler.


I killed my father in that I did not forgive him for wanting me.
I'm a Cancer and my father died of cancer.
We are all murderers but on different
levels and not aware of it.
I've been killing people and giving birth invisibly.
My father trained me to be his opposite, which is why
I attract mass murderers.

Jim is a necrophiliac.
Yes, Jim is real,
I'm positive—
    unless he's using a pseudonym.
You think I made him up?
I have one hundred and six poems
from him that he wrote to me personally.
And he does paintings for me—
a lot of them.

He did a nude painting of me the first time I met him—
a Van Gogh.
He asked me how I wanted to be penetrated.
He wanted to colonize me.

He is also a sculptor though he is working
in the reptile section of a pet store now.
He's going to buy me a puppy and he has three kids.
Mental illness runs in his family.

His last address was Foster Court.
He's an orphan.

He needs a person like me.

He saw me, he met me,
and he immediately wanted to kill me.
I was on Synthroid and I wanted to have sex with everyone I met.
Hashimoto's Thyroid!
That's my disease and that is why I'm a virgin.
The mob needs virgins.
They beg me for forgiveness
so they can skate.
Jim is getting sloppy.
He's the one I let off the hook yesterday.

The level of redemption depends
on the purity of the woman you love.
My father was a hit man
and then he cleaned up his whole life
and all of his sins were forgiven.
That's the way it happens.
He ended up with a house and money for all of us
even though he was a machinist for a hundred dollars a week.
My Grandmother Salvatricia—
all my uncles had to do was ask her forgiveness
and they could skate.

It's the tip of the iceberg.
The mob commits simultaneous crimes.
They frame people so the real crimes go undetected.
They play the odds.

Jim is a picture framer.
That's the code for what he does.
He's learning to play the violin.
It was payment,
if you know what I mean.
He's a necrophiliac because he does not want people
to see his genitals when they are alive.
Everyone assumes that the victims are raped first,
then killed.
But no, they are killed first
and raped later.

Jim committed himself right before he thought he was going
to get caught so he could plead insanity.
While reading Hamlet for the first time he was committed
to the Dodge Building
which is also the name of the building where I work
which is how I forgave him
and why he could skate.

I forgave him
but that was when I found out that he was a necrophiliac
which is why I was committed the second time
last year right before Christmas.
I thought about it
and I threw all of my belongings out of the window
and they came and took me away.
This was the second time but they were amazed
both times at how quickly I pulled myself together.
I pulled out of it.
They just couldn't believe it.
It was like a miraculous recovery.
Twice, of all things. I mean,
just amazing.
So I've had two miraculous recoveries
from mental illness but it's on my record so if there were a trial
I couldn't even take the witness stand.
Actually,
it was the best education I ever received.
I was thinking of going in again
with my guitar because sometimes I had a guitar
and it was very good for the patients.

38

Even the first time, the first time I was there
this one mental patient asked if I was a nurse.
I had everyone ask if I was a nurse both times.
And the doctor who had me committed, after she knew me
for two days, went through more guilt
at having me committed.
I mean she was mortified.
They knew it was all wrong
immediately but they had to keep me for money reasons
and also like if you bring someone into a mental institution
who is not mentally ill, you can get huge
malpractice suits so then
you have to be mentally ill for their records
even if they are wrong.

And this woman was terrified of me!
Both shrinks that I saw, after they stopped seeing me—
both of them were terrified of me.
I mean terrified of me,
okay?

And when I stopped seeing both of them and I would call
and cancel my appointment, one—
she never called me up to like
ask why I stopped going
and the other one called me up once
but he didn't even try to get me back into therapy.
I threatened both of them so much.
Like, I'm the exact kind of person that they need to lock up
right away.
I mean sick!

The second guy I knew was on the verge
of not just saying that I was manic depressive—
which is what they thought I was.
But he was getting into the schizo-affective
disorder kind of stuff.
He was ready to give me all sorts of diseases.
Globus hysteria!

I mean this guy was shaking in his boots,
shaking in his boots
because he knew I would sit there and go on and on
about his problems
and talk about them as if they were mine.
He was just dying.
He was from the Midwest and he was so conservative
but he had a crush on me.
So did the first doctor.
She was a woman.

That was a big problem too.
Like, the crushes had a lot
to do with the whole thing—
why they needed to commit me.
The second guy was married so he couldn't
be attracted to his patients
and the other woman—
she was a woman
so she couldn't be attracted
to a female patient but she got married right after
we started therapy
after I got out of the hospital.
Right away!
Went to Mexico and got married.
That's what I would do if I had feelings like that for a patient.
Think about it.

Just get married right away.

I told her
and I can tell you who was gathered in my bedroom—
you,
and all of the people who conspired to get me there were in the
bedroom
and that's why I had to leave the house—
because they were all in my bedroom.

*You were there.*
*This guy Bill, who sold toys in a toy store—*
*Bill Linn, who is an internationally known psychic.*
*Jim was there.*
*I mean all of the people who know and were in*
*on the conspiracy*
*and there must have been a good dozen or more,*
*okay?*
*Because a lot of people knew.*
*I mean,*
*the number of people conspiring to get me in the hospital*
*was just amazing.*

*I knew this early,*
*before I was committed.*
*I knew all about this.*
*So I've known for three years now. No,*
*two years.*
*But now is the first time I'm not hysterical about it.*
*Do you know what I mean?*
*I went through this whole time thinking maybe I am crazy—*
*yeah, crazy.*

*But now I know that I'm not.*

## MESSAGES

The bird in the tree
is an eye of my enemy.
I find it difficult
to sit quietly.

Although they do not use my name,
there are messages about me
on radio and tv.
I find it difficult to conceal the fact
that I am not angry.

# THE SECOND COMING

I want money—
money for telephones.
Telephones so I can talk to the dead
at home in my spare time,
earn a little extra income
selling fire escapes in the underworld
to shady and disreputable figures
who loathe and despise me
yet must pay the price,
my price,
the only price there has ever been
for fire escapes
which don't work anyway,
I am the first to admit
this to everyone I meet
which is why my wife left me,
which is why I have enemies who will go to any extreme
to blacken my name
and destroy my business by driving customers away
not in droves
but in ordinary taxi cabs never suspecting
that I am still their destination.

There is a roadside chapel you can drive to.
I am nailed to the wall there—
hair sprouted out past all reeling in,
spittle dripping from chin and eyes
that might roll back like the scroll of the sky
on some day of infamy postponed only
if you will listen to me.

There are a thousand things to say to the stranger
who makes the phone in the booth ring
as I walk by, like—It may seem at first
that I am not the one you hoped for.
You may need a shave, a woman,
some gravity to hold you down.

I can provide you
with all of these things.

I've been to Heaven and it's no different.
The dead are risen incorruptible yet soon
pick up the same bad habits they had
when they were alive—

speeding all over drunk and lonely for how it used to be
in the beginningless garden unspoiled by charcoal
briquettes, lighter fluid, a horseman of the apocalypse
astride his riding lawn mower.

I was lonely once too, and broke
with shaking hands trying to light a Camel worried
that I'd light one of my fingers instead.

This is my last cigarette, I said this is my last
cigarette and then  God's voice was in my throat
saying this is my last cigarette
but that's okay.

*It's the one that will burn forever.*

DOGGEREL

When terror bites its bowl and the bone drops
where a dog once stood—only the blurry lines
of an x-ray—the glowing ribs dissolving
into Venus's atmosphere.

He wanted to see what he weighed on other planets.
He wanted to prepare food without
Wearing a hair net.
He wanted to be just like you and me,
don't you see?  This x-ray of a dog
was crying out for love—
blowing up rubber gloves and using them
as hands, seeking out the most human
ways of speaking:  How was his day?
    Ruff!
Did he see the pretty girl curtsey?
    Bow wow!

There was something cruel in the way
he offered himself up as a servant to blind men.
They'd set out together
and only he would return
with tire marks on his leash and a wide smile clenched
around a fat olive wallet with
pink tongue pimento.

He spent the money on radiologists
who set up the screens that let him walk
from scene to scene of his life knowing only
that he showed up on their developing films
to make himself real.  He would do anything—
drink, steal, lie, uncover
avalanche victims only to deny
them the whiskey dangling from his collar
in a little barrel—instead
using it to lure them
into the more distant drifts.

He'd nudge open tourniquets
on the battlefield, nip rattles from
perambulators, picket Laika's lack
of a return ticket, refuse to salivate
when a bell rang, rise up
half in sing half in howl to mourn
the fire trucks going by
to deprive him
of his favorite roasting smell.

*Is this Alpha Centauri?*
He asked the bride he was the groom of
before she tossed her bouquet into the air
and caught it herself unaware that in so doing
she would never be found amidst what was left
of her smoldering gown. The bridesmaids—
who now would never marry—miscarried twins
of themselves, collapsed, and pulsated
as their gowns curled into petals they
were at the whirling center of.

Embarrassed,
my dog buried them and moved on.
          (On Neptune, he weighed 83 pounds.
      On Mars, just 26.)

How to make a dog
that has no meat, no fur yet
maybe sometimes eyes
that materialize to show emotion, reflection,
or that only he (who weighs one thousand
nine hundred and fifty three pounds
on the sun)
has eyes like something fire has seen
and loved too well
and so remained
burning?

I called for him—
my dog of words—
not realizing he'd add a sort of curse
to tilt my picture frame:

*that something alive should come*
*when I call its name.*

I learned to summon first yet
Then how to send away? There's "Go"
but that was too abstract for him to comprehend.
There's pretend-there's-something-in-your-hand-
and-throw-it-yelling-"Fetch!"
Yet he leaves only to come back
with more.
So now I have the dog
and what he returns with—
a ball, or predictable stick.

Yet the highest art must be to summon
something that will make the dog stay,
having forgotten the master—
even if it was his own hand
the master had to throw away. No, the
highest art must be to create a dog
who does the summoning himself—
who brings everything back and chews
what he chooses wisely ignoring
those who would retrieve
and then leave him.

# FURNACE

Revile the swindling pipes—
haunt the accolades.  Paraded
as pets we suck leashes then forget
to heel, forget to lick
the flesh they airbrush out
must go somewhere—a glistening heap
of the lines that define the privacy
of special parts.  Mine
fell off.  Like a leg, I begged it
to make an appointment with
a mimetic prosthetic apothecary approved by
two guys who take the jerking arm off with
a hacking cough or what they saw
yesterday—this girl with removable forepaws—
the little furry kind you'd become furious with
if not for the endearing way
they detach themselves and come right over
when called.  Here boy.  Here
Rover of the haunted plains.  Fetch
this man a magazine of you.
Why
are the best pages stuck
together?

I can hoist my lantern
until the beams spill everywhere—
flow down a woman's long hair
until her breasts heave through a coverlet
to announce that they're there
for me.  I look away shy
with the spying she says, "Your species
can't be trusted.
This is the baby we'll make.
I've already left our wedding for

your wake."

## INTRODUCTION

I either want to have sex with or ingest the entire universe. I wear a sweatshirt copy of the shroud of Turin and sell autographed bibles from every streetcorner often pausing to kick over a plaster lawn burro or expose myself to no one in particular. I know that sleep, sex, and death are identical. I go through the things in my room as if I am already dead. I replace sportsjacket elbow patches with two slices of salami from a sandwich left outside my door. I am euphorically indifferent. I investigate the obvious.

## CUMAEAN SIBYL

The arm I reach for you with has fallen back upon itself—a sleeve with nothing in it undoing even the thread with which it was sewn. Overstuffed puppet propped up to watch scenes running backward, drawers of bureaus closing to leave me undressed upon the breast of my mother dissolving to sea foam. A lover rises from the froth to reassemble me. She wraps a bandage over what once was skin, until it too turned and found a way to burrow in. What is touched will fall away always. Though I am sand pouring through her fingers, she collapses through them to become the ocean floor I fall toward.

## AN APPROPRIATE SONG

The hand that did not obey itself now holds a funeral and quietly buries me. I look through the hymnal. I must find an appropriate song but every page is blank. I notice a broken doll someone has thrown at my feet. I look again and see only dental remains, very much like my own. My hands slide along the pew towards an old woman who has followed the threads too far into a coat that was made for me.

## THE MOUTH I AM THIRSTY FOR

My eye is an eight ounce emerald. My hands grow downward and must sleep. My dreams are like parachutes that open underwater then vanish as clouds  of ink from between the many legs of a woman I follow past neon hotel signs that whisper to one another of the vacancy waiting. Every dark blue umbrella floats by the parking lot where I swim in darkness that pours from my eyes like black candles I swallow with the mouth I am thirsty for.

## ABSENCE

1.  A man hitting an unknown person with a stick.

2.  There is a pause.

3.  A woman has her ovaries removed in the dream of giving birth to her own absence.

4.  Her absence is in the eyes of two farmers, on tractors, in a field as they begin to joust.

5.  It is all becoming clear.

6.  The man, now accused of having sexual organs, will be punished for a crime done.

7.  The woman will have a virtuous son.

## NOTE

A hand.
A hand that returns.
Carrying with it?
A seed, a stone, the secret
of our eventual demise.

One instrument rises to hover
with this hand unlearning
a language of fingertips dripped splat
upon the page—-ageless, enraged
at the paper unpulping to bubble at edges
extending themselves each time
a line draws near.

Look out window and finally notice
everyone in the world staring back.  Must find
a hiding place near the shelves.  Notice:
each thing—whether dust
jacket or paperclip—has a love
of being near the others,
a fear of erasure,
a fond hope.

To be so well enfolded is a joy.
If I press the center of the page it puckers
like a navel and sinks
into the table.
It rises slowly and I press it again—
this time with the tip of a pen.

There's some blood and she's lying there—
the tiny dead table goddess
I dedicate my insincerity to.

Had I been true to her
the blood would have been mine.

## PROLEPSIS

*After swallowing every pill and opening every vein,*
*after seeing that the end of everything is good*
*and that each thing carries its end with it and is delighted*
*when it sees that it is not*
*here at all yet really calling back to itself*
*from what it turned into . . . .*

A final shape shudders back
from certain glimpses into pools. Whatever
thirst needs a well, whatever well
one must descend to. They say it is good luck
to throw the rope in after the bucket has fallen,
that when the needed thing is gone
you might as well be cheerful
about throwing away the rest.

Mouthed utterance of blessings and bequests:
to my furniture I leave the room—
bulbless lamp, undusted mantle, austere chairs
legged and jointed for some mission never galloped off into.
Like them, I tremble and cling against blank skies,
draw curtains to seal the room. It throws off
the aim of the snipers yet won't let the sill
flowers bloom as they should.

The last petals of that year are papers yellowed—
a wrinkled bulb opening to say,
"not my veins, but the veins of a leaf.
I must avoid sunlight."

There seems to be a god who loves idiots—
though he sometimes loves to kill them.
There seems to be a committee of myself scattered
among the brighter moments of my life
like stars badly constellated
in a sky I am to plot my course by.

The first step is away from the light—
white as in all those tacky life after life books.
Lot's wife looks back, jacked deer freeze in the hint of rapture
emitted by a twelve-volt beam, Saint Augustine
names absence the cause of motion. So presence,
complete, will end the uncertainty.


Where everything is, there's no need for memory.
Those revived can barely name
a brilliance that accepts or tosses back,
a special process for turning
nerves' freshly cracked edges to sea glass,
a gift of oil to calm the waves, a gasp
for breath and the fluttering
of new wings in the chest, return of pulse
attended by the last of the light I was allowed to see: a son
radiant, blue-eyed, and as yet unknown to me
in some celestial language joyously beaming,
"Dad, don't be such a fuck-up."

## LETTER

Drifted off after writing her—knew the words would reach her later—water words pouring from the hose he doused the garden with. Something they planted together would grow—he knew this—and that he wasn't innocent of planning the destruction of their lives. She was his lover and would bring her child over to play. He'd tell his wife their guests were here. His wife would be watering her garden too. They moved in and out of houses every few months. There were plenty to choose from. In one of them, he grew old with his lover. In another, he grew old with his wife. The houses were set up as a village wax museum containing posed moments of their lives. His wife drifted in and out of windows throughout the day like slanting sunlight. He could only touch her when enough of her accrued, decanted, unfurled from the clouds of lit dust. This time it was only her shoulder, yet it was enough to push her gently and wish her a lovely voyage among the reeds that sprang up between houses. Now he could visit his favorite scene—the one where his lover's child has finally grown to resemble and reassemble him—his body also of mist twisting in and out of sunlit shapes to please and be stacked by miniature hands carefully arranging.

## POSEIDON

Mere ocean, I confided, there is suicide on the lips of every creature who dares proclaim its love for you. They empty themselves then stack their flasks laughing that the skin stepped out of can be stepped back into again if you are clever enough to befriend what devours you—what washes away all signs of its embrace. You know the type: nervous laughter, saucer-eyed, hands trembling rabbit-hopeful they can dart back up their sleeves, lying awake at night grieving the loss of embossed seals that once held the scroll together. It unfurls like a sail— revealing what held you in place to the wind. One puff and its over: the waterfall, the whirlpool, whichever edge of the world one wandered too near. Shipwrecked, you beachcomb for shells to use as the ears roaring always to call you back.

## BECAUSE OF THESE THINGS

One thousand times I told them I was not the one they were looking for and one thousand times they told me that I was. On a Sunday morning three years ago no one in the whole goddamn town knew what was going to happen. I knew what was going to happen because I was about to do that which was about to be done by none other than me. On a cloudless day the onlookers looked on in horror and with apparent indifference as I circled above them in a Belgian airplane proclaiming myself to be none other than he who had risen—

Above them in an airplane. He who circled above them, he who would fly away from that town so fast that their heads would spin. And their heads did spin. Which is why I became confused and why I am where I am today without an airplane or money to buy an airplane with, without a crowd to fly over, without anything whatsoever at all.

EVENING

On the shore, desire for the stars to fall.

All of them from the sky, darkness

until I look to the ocean floor where slowly,

the stars reassemble.

(I am the one who has drowned)

## EXPLANATION

When there's a tin can lying on the ground near a dog, it's not the dog attacking you—it's the tin can controlling the dog. The dog itself—roasting its skin off as ribs quiver and widen, is being burned in a campfire because of the can. The can itself is the object of suspicion—the one thing in any landscape or scene that is secretly fake and is placed as a clue to those who may then discover the entire landscape or scene is fake. The only way to escape is to destroy what the one fake thing is controlling. The fake thing will disappear, but then you have to go away too—to a new place where everything is fake until you notice the one thing that is real. . . .

# EYELET

A knitting needle collapses into the lap
of all that had hoped to live yet ended
up hypnotized: a grandmother
who has forgotten her life so must knit one
without purling two—her pattern unfurling
around her like a flag of loss.

Yet renewal is not far off.
They've routed the fallen yarn around a spool that turns—
one shudder for each stitch.   A slight recoil
at the thought of all the scarves that could have been
spun out by those spidery hands.

She's delighted to rock and unravel
in the fisherman's boat of her astonished chair—
a pleasant nod to the ladies below who tie
the tiny knots and set her lines.

# PROPOSAL FOR A THIRD WIFE

Should you light upon my ruined lawn—
Freshly flown in, I would salt
Your wings and eat them.
As I flattered you
the chains would form.

From inside a drained fountain,
I'd mold casings and pour
A compliment of cement over your feet
Then you'd need me
To help you walk inside. I'd show
You floors to clean,
Special slippers to wear
Over your cement blocks so
They wouldn't scratch the finish.

Our bedroom is on the third floor.
You'll pass portraits of my last wives, expended.
Be sure to warmly greet the children
Who fly past when they hear the familiar thunder
Of blocked feet ascending.
Forgive them,
Yet they've heard the noises you'll make.

Here's the bed. The wings,
I'll give back to you in a special form,
Digested, synthesized, injected
Suddenly between your legs spread
In a way that reminds us
You were once capable of flight.

You mustn't move.
As you pose for your portrait,
The slow takeover begins from within you—
Unfolding limbs, dividing cells
Modeled on the one
I've devised for you.

On the day your womb outweighs those blocks
I'll chisel them off yelling, Freedom!

From this prison that will outlast
The cries of all who pass through it,
Something worthwhile will emerge
To end your chrysalid state—

A daughter patterned
To continue this game.
I'll set her on you to prey
And to drain

You to a shell—
Mere container for
Whatever I pour into you.

I'm not sure why I do this.
And, by the way,
You have such lovely eyes,
Such fine legs I'd follow anywhere
If only they weren't so very tired.

VOW

Once hinged, the door
abhors its frame.
It shudders shut
inflamed by doubts
and casuistry—this
winnowing down of possibilities
for a geometric plane that could
span sawhorses, ramp velocipedes, or fly
bolted as wing to Messerschmitt
in full dive now pulling up
to stall and plummet
once again.


Though I use you for this,
some might claim you are not
a woman at all, but a membrane
to be penetrated by the lonely
in their time of need.
I posit my deference deep
within you. Should
our bodies fail
to uncouple through years
of joy or tearful welling, I swear
to open you reverently again
and again without closing.

DECEMBER 1,

Lower-back pain began again today.
My one true love
is gone.
I masturbate gloomily near a pile of worthless lottery tickets.
I have started to drink.
I would end it all;
however,
I have purchased a book on extraterrestrials.
They will bring joy soon.

## SUNLIGHT FLOODS THE ROOM.
## THREE ARE DROWNED.

I am out of sight
I am out of mind
I sadly fear my mittens
I am lost

The sign says—DON'T WALK
I crawl across the street
The secrets I think of
Begin to think of me

I am the man on the window ledge
Who jumps out the window for some air
I am not an actor
But I play one on tv

I feed the hand that bites me,
Feed gravy-soaked sponges to every dog
I have created god in my own image
He approves of this

## BEAUTY

Blueberry spies often watch me from their windowsills then vanish across the empty highways. Supermarket vegetables pushing carts toward the end of an aisle that gets farther and farther away. The melon claims to be Alfred Lord Tennyson. I am a half-human deity with the hind legs of a goat. Apocalypse butterflies flood the supermarket aisles. We try. We can no longer see the terrible endlessness. We thank the butterflies. The butterflies thank us for imagining them.

## NARCISSUS

Door closed,
I hear blue-veined feet spinning scale dials that spin
up to less and less.

She cloaks herself in mohair sweaters
while shaving the downy lanugo hair of her own.
Today she shaved her eyebrows off,
just because. So mother propped her
topless before the reflection of withered
hanging breasts
and skin tightly drawn over bone.

When we visit she says, "I want to come home."
"It's simple," her little brother says. "Just eat."
Like the Irish to their famined,
we bring lilacs
to cover the rich dying smell
she leaves.

# FEAST OF THE ASSUMPTION

A Roman emperor of the same name
flies over at great speed as days eat inwardly
toward no goal at all but the squalling
of tempests brought in from distant bays to swirl
miniaturized in tureens no ladle need stir.

The domestic fury contained
in hors d'oeuvres will one day cause them to rise up
and observe—among other things—
the care with which they were made.
It is apparent in their workmanship—
a state of repose that lies still having perfectly gathered
the motion which preceded it.

They are presented on a tray
offered to guests unsuspecting
that consumption replaces their cells
with a host, accepted as symbol,
now insistent upon fact.

As landscapes sway through wineglasses to torment them,
they mourn their old lives a moment before bursting
as gastronomes, or,
if without sin,
erupting into laughter at newborn limbs
outstretched to clutch, eyes
dissolving into what they see:

Mary ascending attended by seraphim
wrapped in clouds shrouding
this virgin—the virgin of anything
that never happened until it was seen
and in seeing was born, lived, died.

So in bearing she unbore him
to float crucified in her womb—
a sad walrus of himself knowing even then
how it always ends when the wise follow
a starlit path.

# PHOTO ALBUM

We are screaming and we are swimming near grass
of the graves that grew above the lives we planted
each day hoping that the shutter and flash would capture
what all of the gestures added up to when they were taken away
by page upon page of inflated pools overlaid
by burning birthday cakes, kids flying off
swingsets over grandmothers climbing stepladders
to hang birdhouses next to wedding gowns.

*The drowned boy will always be four*
*in a last picture with his face against the sliding glass door.*
*When everyone was asleep he slipped from cottage to dock*
*and walked out of his life.*

My wife and I will be floating happily inside the brandy glass
where a department store photographer placed our heads.
We could have gotten the star background
but preferred to drown forever
in the moving spirits distilled from still memory.

*If we are containers that contain ourselves,*
*if we are waiting on shelves to fall off,*
*defeat is as easy as never being able to see—*
*how we were smashed and what we were attached to,*
*who called our name and changed us*
*into each other and us all.*

Gather dolls, squalling infants, clippings
of the fire that destroyed the Masonic Lodge, the daughters'
daughters, pet dogs, favorite coffins
and the first moon a child sees out the window
as she's riding in a car....

*It glows and follows to show that even it is alive.*

Add stepmother's goldfish, a half-wit nephew,
brothers' lovers, a picnic basket on the lap
of the homosexual astrologer
with a cat born on Hitler's birthday.

*there is a flash as we all remember*
*and are preserved in each other's embrace.*

And a lingering, dumb prayer sent back fourteen years to the fifth page
where the neighbor's son woke up before anyone—

May there have been enough light at dawn for you  to look down
into the water and see the reflection of the sky you were stepping into
instead of a boat.

.

# THE SECRET ORDER OF THE WEEPING PINE

Spinsters splinter wood in winter.
Smoke from ashes rises.
The wind blows black and far away
an idiot hypnotizes his wristwatch—
makes it leap into a glass of water
and say things it will later regret.

Regret begets regretters
knitting sweaters near fires
enkindled by the wrath of widowless
squires. Their wives live on—
though long dead to them, devoted
to overcoats, ghostly,
trembling where they hang—
awaiting the sudden plunge of limbs
stuck in them to swish away
again.

Above a curled-open tin,
a wife dreams of misery revoked
by tea cozies and clean counters—
a meal with all of the usual trappings,
ensnared guests, the din
of compulsory toasts.

Her husband suspects his glass
of water contains the ocean,
that his watch is all of time.
The brine of memory torments him
to hammer-tap and corrode all that ticks
and plays tricks upon his senses,
to swat at defenseless vermin shaped
like children ill with plagues devised
by deities that punish only
the kneeling few who praise them.

He knows that geodes must be cracked
open to sparkle, that birds must leave their branches
to fly, that humanity must be smashed
like a china cabinet to end the customary toll
of time without a face or hands among the
swirl of tiny gears he understands will sate his thirst
if he is brave enough to drink.

# HYPNOGOGIC

They no longer creep so closely as they once did—
The mouths swallowing mouths beneath closed lids
Noses smelling noses, tongues tasting tongues—
Lapping like waves upon a shore of all oceans
The creatures washed up share a limb made of limbs
And an eye of all the eyes that have ever been

Our skin the sand spreading on and on—
This is where we've gone accidentally and forever
Beyond our lives and what they led to—
A confusion of the parts that want to want to be sewn back
Into the bodies that have tossed them here

*I have seen it,* I want to shout
*And it has made me quiet for years*
Of gathering parts and finding for each its place
Of hoping for words that won't erase themselves
Of embracing my children, their hands attached without seam
In a world I am not dreaming.

## MUSICIAN

Once hammered bright the thin
threnody trilled ambulative among
the notes hit. He built a spigot
for his blood to pour from.
He thumped a trident in time
with the crowd's roar.
He took vegetation to mean
planks indented by teeth,
chewed on by civilizations that rise
and fall in four-four time dissolved
into rising seas, coated with brine
and barnacle if dipped at all
into the glossy froth of audience.

Ah, how the centuries pass
through the singing eyelet that spews
spun thread we can still wear if
we divide endlessly this moment to see
we aren't here at all but are calling back to ourselves
from frames arranged to show first steps,
attempts at courtship, circumstantial pomp,
the shallow graves we fall into
and crawl from each day praising
the passage of time—
its signature embroidered only
when the last note rises perfectly to consume all those
who came before,
when one moment passes
to another moment the secret—
we are the same.

## SCALE

Hoist an eye to the highest branch.
String no line to telegraph back
the things you've seen by rising first
to these heights lit not
by sunlight or lantern swaying
yet by the glow that gathers
around a scene well seen.

The figure model disrobing before an easel—
how vision flies out to meet the startled landscape.
Fruit falling from trees as they reach into the sky,
Union soldiers splayed and gaping just in time
for the invention of photography.

Flash powder and sun's rays dim
next to the light we pour out of
our eyes and the world
pours back.

It whelms,
lays bare, knocks flat

Or enters the eye and exits through fingers
shaping mouths in clay, pressing string
to fret, dragging pen over white
expanses we stumble across.

Staggering loss
or merely loss that limps away—
disheveled, it lives to see  another day and rises
to robe itself again.  Beauty's friend, loss
that reminds, that makes us name:

*God is lamp post, is grain of sand,*
*is bathroom mirror.*

Or:

*My vision is failing,*
*my liver is bad, my wife is gone.*

I was trying to shave and couldn't tell
nose from cheek. I heard laugh
turn to whimper turn to howl
I turned
to see who was making this sound.
It was me—above or outside
or beside myself,
fulfilling grief's cliché.

*There is a limit to pain and you are taken away*

Bless shock, the way wreckage is scattered
across a landscape too vast to survey,
the moment of accident
forgotten,
whatever ocean opened
and poured in that day
to let me howl and cry beyond
words at first, then—
My god-damned doctor, my MRI.

What didn't kill me was distilled—
turned to memory and filed beside
those who had loved and fallen from
even higher—

Bridesmaids whispering, Brueghel's corpses,
long ago a child who asked
*What are you afraid of?* I said *heights.*
*Well, just imagine that I'm a height,*
she said not knowing how soon she'd fall,
how terribly beautiful she was.

## SHELLEY

Sleep with oceans, if at all
and by the light that blinds you know
what shores wash up upon themselves
only to rise slowly and reclaim

forever the same secret forgotten
so we may live to see joy in what does not destroy us
yet glimmers with a final light we approach
and fall back from.

Hipassus of Metapontum thought of numbers that went on and on
irrationally—repeating decimals
like arrows that could reach heaven.
When he went to sea he was drowned—
though whether by the Gods or his colleagues
is a matter of some debate.

It has always been dangerous to think this way—
to row out so far that returning
seems like a small bay where everyone is waving goodbye—
dividing up your possessions, moving into your house. . . .

If you find treasure, you can buy your things back
but the more treasure you gather,
the more you'll want to stay.
There are thousands of you washing up each day—
the ones who saw things they could not return from—
their drowned bodies waiting to be burned—
a promised land glittering like wreckage in their eyes.

## ONE

He said our thoughts are like crows upon the horizon.
Some stay in their trees and wait for us to notice them.
Others fly away forever. And so what—
There is a place where the forgotten things gather
Outside of skin and the definitions
That try to keep us here. Everything is seen
And remembered.

A dead bird with its wings outspread upon the water,
A fallen tree with its shivering limbs.
These things that vanish—We say goodbye to them again
Until the only thing to say goodbye to
Is saying goodbye.

From far enough away, they look as if they are one—
All we have thought and done and forgotten.
I walk toward all of this hoping for a horizon that at last
Does not recede as I approach it.

## PSALM

                He spent his life noticing

The tyranny of line,

                sleeves

        dropping down.

                grievous in the way

          Pages turn,

                their fabric is slit to

        drip rivulets,

                allow palms protrusion,

        spilling texts—

                into the open air

a procession bleeding,

                where they grasp

lurching for words to hurl

                at things unimaginable

inside the worlds of themselves,

                until they are set down,

        alone, to fray—

                unraveling is how we will say,

        what wove us

                "to shuttle back through looms,

      to fill the once empty

                caress of interlacing

      moments forming

                thread that suspends us

     if we ever touched,

                if we can trace these lines back through

     each other's skin."

Acknowledgments

*Asylum*:
"The Mouth I Am Thirsty For"

Café Review:
"Prolepsis"

*Dogzplot & Paragraph:*
"Explanation" (different versions separated by many years)

*Evergreen Review*:
"The Second Coming"

*Fine Madness*:
"Golden Rule," "Messages," "Relationship,"
"Yellow Line," "Teaching Cooking Skills, Purdy Group Home"

*Grand Street*:
"Anastasia, Purdy Group Home," "A Translation, Purdy Group
Home," "Divining," "Flight," "Mathematician," "Moth Moon,"
"Sunlight Floods the Room. Three Are Drowned."

*62 New Hampshire Poets*:
"Rorschach Test"

*Publishing Genius:*
"The Tip of the Iceberg"

Special thanks to **Baltimore Is Reads** for plastering my poems all
over telephone poles & to **Contre Coup Press** for a letterpress
chapbook entitled **Schizophrenomania**.

Please search the internet for:
**Matt Jasper: A Collection of Bad Poetry**
(I suggested themes and many lines and then hired Tao Lin etc. to
write for me at $2 per poem). In the future, I hope to hire people to
write all of my poems for me. If you would like to be employed in
this manner, please email me at: mattjasper555@hotmail.com. I also
accept fan and hate mail at this address.

Please listen to my band (Pneumershonic) online at WFMU.

*Many thanks to Rachel Wakefield, Lisa Carver, Jarid Del Deo, Charles
Simic (who wrote that I was a genius once and then regretted it),
Mekeel McBride, Mimi White, Russell Edson, the ghost of Robert
Burton, Mom & Pop, and Albion, Eudora, Will, and Max.*

Matt Jasper was born in Manhattan in 1966. A frequent contributor to *Rollerderby* and *Grand Street* in the 90s, he went on to have many children and start a poorly-posed-taxidermy-and-bad-yard-sale-art-themed restaurant called the Friendly Toast. He collects schizophrenic autobiographies and makes lists of poet enemies in Farmington, New Hampshire. He is currently working on a book-length poem entitled *Obolus*.